# Love Yourself

*Complete Guide to "Self-Love,"
Life Healing and Building your
Self-Esteem*

**Jeffrey Turpen**

# Summary

You have to look at what you are getting out of your life if you want to stand out and make it worth living. You must know how to improve upon your self-esteem.

This book is all about helping you to see how you can build that self-esteem to grow into a better person. You will learn in this guide about how you can help yourself by being alongside positive people and avoiding comparisons. You will also see why having new experiences in your life on a regular basis can change your life for the better.

The points in this guide are all very practical and simple to use. More importantly, they give you a perfect idea of what to do in your life to make it stronger.

**Your Gift!**

We want to show our appreciation that you support our work, so we have put together a gift for you.

Just visit the link on the last page of this book to download it now.

We know you will love this gift.

Thanks!

# Table of Content

# Introduction

*"Having low self-esteem is like driving through life with the hand-brake on."*

*– Maxwell Maltz*

We all feel down in our lives every once in a while. We do everything we can to make ourselves feel happy and comfortable with our lives. But even with all that, it is still a challenge to try and make our lives as great as they could be.

It is a necessity for all of us to think about the things we can for improving our lives and making them feel stronger and better. This guide is all about helping you to understand what you can do to give your life a greater sense of purpose.

You will learn in this simple guide the many things that can be done to restore your self-esteem and heal your life. As you will explore here, it is not too difficult to get the most out of your mind and your life.

It is especially critical for you to look into what you can do to restore your life and give your self-esteem the boost it needs. When you feel better about yourself, your life becomes a little easier. You will not try and make things all the more challenging than they have to be. You will certainly feel confident about who you are without dragging yourself down any paths that might be harmful or dangerous.

Your emotions will also be easier to control when you have the self-esteem you require. You will not feel as though you are letting yourself or other people down.

It will be easier for you to have better relationships with other people as well. The general public prefers individuals who feel positive about themselves. They want those who are ready to do anything and aren't afraid of themselves.

More importantly, you will feel happier about yourself when you have enough self-esteem in your life. There's no reason why you should feel upset with your life. As you improving upon your attitude for life, you will find that it's not all that hard for you to get the most out of your everyday experience.

# Chapter 1 – Avoiding Comparisons

*"Judgment traps you within the limitations of your comparisons. It inhibits freedom."*

*– Willie Stargell*

One of the greatest reasons why so many people struggle with their lives is because they are constantly trying to compare themselves with others. Some like to compare themselves because they want to think that they are as good as others.

It is natural for all of us to compare ourselves to other people. We all have our own heroes or idols that we love to follow. But sometimes we get far too caught up in those things. We start to think far too much about people and what they are like.

We all like to compare ourselves with all of these people because we think they are all better than us and appealing in some way.

But when we do this, we struggle to look at the big picture.

It only takes a few thoughts or observations of other people to start getting the wrong idea over what can be done in life to make it stand out.

But the truth is that you cannot compare yourself to other people all the time. Think about it for a moment. Let's say that you like to play baseball. You want to try and build your skills up to where you can be the next big name baseball player.

But no matter what you do, you might struggle to be a big star. You might try and work yourself to death just to try and make it onto a particular team.

It can be difficult to think about how you're not as good as baseball as other people are. That does not mean that you should be comparing yourself all the time.

Not everyone who plays baseball can hit a ball as hard as Aaron Judge. Most certainly can't throw a ball as fast as Max Scherzer can. They might not be able to make the smartest managerial decisions like Mike Matheny or Joe Maddon could. More importantly, you will feel as though you are not willing to let yourself be who you truly are if you compare yourself to others all the time.

You will not feel all that comfortable with who you are in general when you keep on comparing yourself with others in some way.

Simply put, you have to stop comparing yourself to other people all the time. Everyone has their strengths. You just need to think about yours, which leads us to the next topic.

## *Look At Your Strengths*

When you work to improve your life, you have to think about your strengths. Look at what you do for a living and think about how you might excel in certain things.

Everyone has skills that make them great at something. Some people might be talented writers who have a way with words. Others can fix up all sorts of vehicles.

Look at the strengths you have and see what you can do to build upon them or to use them to your advantage. If you are good with cars then maybe you could consider working at a vehicle repair shop. Maybe you could go to a technical education program to learn how to work with commercial vehicles or high-end vehicles from Maserati or Ferrari among others. The potential for you to go far with your skills is endless when you know what you are great at or when you build upon those abilities.

Think about those strengths that you have in your life and see what you can do to move forward with them. You might be surprised when you think about what you are good at and work on those things in particular.

As you look at those strengths, you will be free to be who you truly are. You won't be limited to trying to be like someone you are not. Instead, you are blazing your trail as you stick with those positives. It makes your life all the more worthwhile when considered right.

## *Focus on Being Good Enough*

You should not assume that you have to be perfect in everything you do in your life. Perfection is something that no one can ever truly accomplish.

Rather, you should think about being good enough for whatever it is you are doing. Look at how you are working on your goals and how you are moving closer to completing them.

For instance, you might have a desire to be a car technician. You could study at a vocational school and complete your tests to be certified. After this, you would find a great job with a quality repair shop or another place that could use your services.

Don't think that you have to be perfect in every aspect of your work. Instead, think more about what you can do to pass your exams. Look at how you're going to work on different vehicles at the start of your career.

You have to think less about perfection and more about what's coming in the here and now. When you complete your exams and find a job, you will see that you truly are good enough to be where you want to be.

Of course, you can use this as a stepping stone to a much greater objective like working for a distinct group or taking care of unique cars that might be a little fancier. But whatever the case is, everything you do must be done gradually without forcing yourself into situations that might be too tough to get into.

Keeping your life organized and in check can truly be helpful. Be certain when looking at your life that you think carefully about how well you are not likely to lose control of it all. Avoid thinking that everything has to work as well as possible. Focus more on being positive with your life while looking at what you could do to move forward in any manner.

More importantly, avoiding perfection is critical in that reality can get in the way of this concept. You might think you have to do things in a certain way, but in reality, you would end up having problems happen that cause you to think bad things. As you stick with a better mindset, you will find that your life is indeed worthwhile. You will not be a slave to your own mind as you start to get on your way to happiness. More importantly, you will not feel as though you cannot go anywhere in your life.

Be ready to think for yourself. It makes a world of difference when you see what makes your life stand out and powerful.

## Chapter 2 – Avoid Your Inner Critic

"Watch for the joy-stealers: Gossip, criticism, fault-finding and a negative, judgmental attitude." Joyce Meyer

The next reason why so many people don't have enough self-esteem in their lives is that they think they need to do everything to be perfect. They keep listening to their inner critics.It does not take much for you to focus on your inner critic.

While it is true that the voice you hear in your head might help encourage you to do things and to get up and at them, there are also times when that voice might be problematic. It might say that you're not doing things right or that you are lazy. It could be critical of you as someone who is worse off than other people.

The bad things that your inner voice will tell you can be difficult to bear with in your life. But that does not mean you have to listen to that critic all the time.

## *Tell Your Voice To Stop*

As you hear negative things in your mind, you will have to think about telling your inner voice to stop. But that doesn't mean you should just tell your voice to stop it directly. You have to plan yourself when getting that inner critic to get out of your life.

The best thing to do is to create a stop-word. Such a term is a word that you can use to tell your inner critic to get away and to stop bothering you.

That stop-word could be anything you want it to be. You could say something like "Not today" or "We're not going there." Anything that is memorable always works.

Feel free to try as many of these words or phrases as you want. The key is to think of something that will stop your critic from moving forward and regularly yelling at you.

*Refocusing*

Think about what you can do next after you get that inner critic to stop. Turn your focus to something new.

Look at something you could think about that might be more constructive. You have to choice to follow something you love or maybe a new experience that might prove to be your new favorite. Being ready to think about the good things in life is always a positive to get into.

Reflect on an event that is coming up or something you want to do later on in the day. Consider the many things in your life that are productive and helpful. Whatever the case is, think about things that are productive and worthwhile in your life. Look less at the negative things in your life and more about what makes it worthwhile. Take a careful look at how you are feeling and what you could do to give yourself the control you need in your life. The powerful attitude that you come across in your mind will give you the help you need to make the change in your life that is needed for it to be worthwhile.

## *How Would Friends Help You?*

When you feel down and critical of yourself, look at what your friends might do. The odds are they have their ideas on what you should do.

One thing is for certain in that your friends would be happy to help you and give you the encouragement you need. They love to give you the emotional assistance you need.

Put yourself in the shoes of someone who is close to you. What would that person do for you? What would you do for that fellow?

You will have more than enough help as you look at the people around you. Look at what they can do for you and find a way to make it so they will give you the help you require for having a more productive and controlled life.

## Be Constructive

You should look at what you are doing in your life and take pride in everything you are doing. Reflect upon what you do and see what makes it so beneficial in your mind.

More importantly, you have to be as constructive as possible as you take pride in your work. Look at what you have been doing and focus on what you feel makes it great. Use those points to think about how you can improve upon other things in your life.

Don't ever dwell upon what people might tell you. Even when people say that you are not doing much, you should still be positive in any manner. Besides, you could compare your positives with the negatives that people feel about you and use your beneficial aspects to correct those problems. When you think this way, you will find that it is not all that hard for your life to move forward and stay strong.

Think about what you have been doing in your life and consider what can be done to improve upon your goals later on.

For instance, look at how you perform your job and review the skills that you use the most. Take those skills and find ways to use them to improve upon any flaws that you might hold. You'll find that there is always a way for you to succeed and be strong.

All people with self-esteem know that they shouldn't take any negative words too hard. Even the best people out there have had their own critics. There are probably several film critics out there who have ridiculed Leonardo DiCaprio a number of times for his acting roles. But if he listened to them and got himself down instead of being constructive, he wouldn't be able to improve upon his work and become a popular and highly-paid actor.

Being constructive in your life is a necessity. It keeps you from listening to that voice in your head. It also gives you more of a focus on what you know is worthwhile and can make a difference in your life.

# Chapter 3 – Motivate Yourself the Right Way

*"Ability is what you are capable of. Motivation determines what you do. Attitude determines how well you do it."*
*– Lou Holtz*

Some people think that they can heal their lives by thinking about positive stuff. That is an honest statement in that there are plenty of great things in your life that are worth reviewing.

But before you try to motivate yourself, you have to look at what you are doing to make it work.

You must motivate yourself carefully. You have to look properly to see how well you are thinking about your life and what you are aiming to get out of it.

As you do this, your attitude will improve. You will feel ready to take on the world and use your abilities to your greatest possible potential. This is all about going far and being more worthwhile in the long run without feeling as though someone is going to judge you for any reason.

## Analyze the Benefits of Good Things

You might think about lots of good things in your life. Whatever you are thinking about, look at the benefits that can come through.

There are always going to be some great positives coming out of your life.

For instance, you might feel motivated about a vacation that you are trying to save up your money for so you can enjoy a great time in some new far-off place. You could develop the positive self-esteem needed to help you get to your job to earn money to pay for that vacation.

As you think about that vacation, you should look at the benefits that come with it.

These include benefits relating to not only getting away from your responsibilities for a bit but also for seeing new things or experiencing special activities.

You could even think about spending time with the people who will come to your trip with you.

Focusing on all the great things that will come about in the future when you get into something you want is always great. It helps you see the big picture with regards to what makes life so worthwhile.

### Think About What You Like

As you motivate yourself, look at what you enjoy doing in your life. Look at the things that you are interested in and what you might like in particular. You might find that motivation will come around quickly when you think about the stuff in your life that makes you happy above all else.

When you are enthusiastic about what you are motivated by, you will find that any inner critics in your mind will be pushed aside. With this in mind, you must think about what you like doing and how you are improving your life in some manner. Motivation can make a world of difference if handled right. Be certain when motivating yourself that you look at what makes the things you are thinking about all the more valuable.

# Chapter 4 – Relax For a Moment

*"If a man insisted always on being serious, and never allowed himself a bit of fun and relaxation, he would go mad or become unstable without knowing it."*

*- Herodotus*

It's one thing for people to tell you to relax for a moment. It's another thing actually to do it. But when you can do it right, you will find that it is not all that hard for you to feel great about yourself.

The best way to relax is to think for yourself about what makes your life worthwhile. Just spend a few minutes thinking about yourself and what makes you a great person. You will find after a while that it is not all that hard to stay upbeat.

You have to slow down for a bit and take some deep breaths each day. As you do this, you have to ask yourself what you appreciate about yourself.

Think for a bit while relaxing about what makes you feel happy. Look at what you think is ideal for your life and what makes it so beneficial.

Look at all the great things that you have put into your life. Ask about how you can get people to laugh and forget about their problems.

Just look at everything in your life that you know is worthwhile. Don't just think about the biggest details. Look back at the small stuff in your life. Anything that is useful and positive in your life should become a factor in your life no matter how minute the point might be.

As you think about these things while you relax, you will find that you are indeed a great person and that there is nothing that you cannot do. You will get rid of the negativity in your life if you just think about what makes it useful.

Remember to rest for a bit and think about what you are getting into in your life every once in a while. As you stop and collect yourself, you will begin to notice that there is no real reason as to why you should feel uncomfortable with whatever it is you are doing for yourself.

# Chapter 5 – Be Reflective

"The heart is the best reflective thinker." –Wendell Phillips
Reflecting upon your life is always great to do. You will find that there are always good things to think about and that you are doing things right in some manner.

As you look at the great things that can come about in your life, you will see that there is always something worth looking forward to. Keeping a strong perspective on what you are doing and how you are moving forward with your life will make a world of difference regarding helping you go far and being stronger.

For instance, you could be happy with how you got out of bed on time. That happiness continues as you get to work on time and then as you have a good day on the job where the time moves fast and you don't have anything stressful happening. Your life will start to improve as you reflect upon everything good that happens. The changes in your life eventually lead to the big point that you need to look into – the fact that sometimes the smallest things in life can make a big difference.

## *Look At the Small Victories*

Think more about the small victories that come about in your life. You might see that things are better than you expect them to be.

Here's an example of how you can be reflective with regards to those small victories. Let's say that you just started up a sports team in some form. Naturally, your new team might not be all that good because you have a bunch of players who have never been together on the same side before and a new organization that you will have on your side.

You might struggle at the start. But when you look at some of the great things you are doing, you will see that you are doing things right. When you start to train players and they start to get along with each other, you will feel as though you have attained a small victory. The moves you make and the changes that come along means that the players are doing well with one another and that they are ready to play together and win. Over time the positives that come with running your team will start to increase. You will feel as though the only way to move forward with your team is up.

Whether it entails a small amateur team or some group competing around the country, your team will grow if you are positive. Thinking about the great things that come along helps to keep you motivated.

It might take a while, but it will help you to move forward and be positive. After all, the Miami Marlins didn't win a few baseball championships overnight. They had to spend years and add up all the small victories over time to reach the largest ones.

Be progressive and thoughtful about what you are doing in your life. Think about the things that will occur in your life and look at what will make them stand out while giving you the help you demand.

# Chapter 6 – Break Out of Your Mold

*"Variety is the soul of pleasure."*
*– Aphra Behn*

Everyone likes to try new things every once in a while. It is important that we spice up our lives now and then and try things that you have never done before.

Variety is always something that is worthwhile. Look at David Bowie's musical career, and you will see that it contains all kinds of music that were drawn from a variety of inspirations. He clearly knew that to stand out and be positive about his music career he needed to mix his work up and show that he could do anything. It is no wonder why people still admire his music to this day.

Another musician to consider is Elvis Presley. He made not only various rock and roll music records but also some country and gospel works.

He was happy with the variety of music that he produced and always knew that there was something for him to enjoy performing. That positive attitude helped him to become a star who still has a massive following of devoted fans decades after his death.

You could learn quite a bit from these points. You should be willing to break out of your mold and think about the many things you could do with your life. Look at the new experiences that can come out of your life and find ways to incorporate them into anything you want to do.

You will have the self-esteem you require when you add a bit of variety to your life. The positivity of variety comes as you will have more things to look forward to getting along with. Life will not be the same old drag that it might be now if you just add some new stuff here and there.

Break out of your mold. Add something special into your life. Take in a new experience that you've never been a part of. The odds are you will find something new that you are bound to love and enjoy. Maybe you might find a particular skill that you never knew you have.

No matter what it is you like, you must be ready to move forward and do something new and spectacular. You need to look at how well your life is being run and how you can add something outstanding to your life so you will feel great about what you want to do in your life.

***Getting Out of Your Comfort Zone***

The most important reason why it is so important to get out of your routine is that you will feel better about the outside world. You have to get out of your comfort zone every once in a while.

When you escape your routine, you will start to feel as though there is nothing you cannot do. You will be ready to try new things and see if you like them.

The most important point is that you don't expect far too much to come out of what you are doing. Remember that getting into new experiences is all about seeing what is out there. It is all about self-discovery and thinking about what could be right for you. A positive mindset gives you the self-esteem boost that you require.

Be ready to get out of the same ordinary things that you are stuck in. Do not be afraid of what might happen. The excitement of life is there for the taking. It is up to you to go after what you are interested in getting. Being in new events and experiences improves upon your self-esteem as you will feel confident and unafraid of what might come across in any situation.

# Chapter 7 – Be Around Good People

*"You should appreciate the goodness around you, and surround yourself with positive people."*

*– Nadia Comaneci*

Sometimes the company that you keep makes a great impact on your life. When you are around those who are positive, you will start to feel upbeat and encouraged. Meanwhile, anyone who is not so happy does nothing but hurt your mind and attitude.

Have you ever been around someone in the workplace who always complained about things and was not all that happy? Maybe you might have wanted to get away from that person. You probably felt that way because you don't want to be around someone who isn't all that confident or comfortable about your situation.

You must surround yourself with good people that you can feel comfortable with. Think less about how familiar they are and more about their attitudes.

After all, every person in the world has had some support system to succeed. If Cal Ripken Jr. didn't have a family that supported his baseball dreams or team members who weren't behind him, then he would not have held the desire to keep showing up for baseball games day in and day out. Do you really think he would have played in so many games in a row if he surrounded himself with negative-thinking people?

You too can go far if you are around the right people all the time. Whether it entails completing an educational degree or just getting to work on a regular basis, you have to be around people who aren't afraid to be around you. But you have to understand who you should be avoiding.

## *Who To Avoid*

Do not be around people who try to be overly perfect. Those perfectionists are people who might be too demanding. They are hard to themselves and do not know what to do when they fail or struggle in some way.

Avoid those who are overly critical. It is one thing to be around a person who is optimistic and willing to give you advice on how to fix any problems that come about in your life. It is another to be around someone who calls you names, mocks you for what you are doing and thinks less of you for what you are doing.

Those who are not willing to support you are not your friends. You don't want to be stuck with people who certainly don't have much concern for you in any manner.

It is predictable for people to be pessimistic these days. With so many people being overly cynical about the world, it does not take much for people to feel downbeat. Make sure you avoid being around those who might be hard and difficult to be around. This is all about keeping your mind at ease while ensuring that you are not stuck with those who do not have much worry about what you are doing in life.

## *Who To Be Around*

Naturally, you might think you need to be around people who are the exact opposite of what you have just read about. While this is certainly true, there are several things that you have to look into in particular.

Be with people who are always looking on the sunny side of life. Hang around those who are capable of finding silver linings in anything that might come about. As you will learn from these people, there is always something worthwhile in life that makes it ideal.

Stick around those who are lenient and are not afraid of failure. Be with those who want to learn more about who such people are truly supposed to be like while trying new things. These are people who know that nobody in the world is ever truly perfect. They are ready to do more with others without being hard on themselves or other people in general.

Always be around those who are never judgmental, aren't afraid of imperfection and know how to be happy. Sometimes the great feelings that you will come across will make a correct world of difference.

Besides, it is often easier for you to have a stronger life if you think more about the good things that can come about over time. You need to have a great support system to go far in life. Do not be afraid to look around and find people who care for you and want you to succeed. You might meet some great new friends in the process who want you to get the self-esteem that you require for the best possible life you could ever ask for.

# Conclusion

You might be surprised at what you can get out of your life when you just think about yourself. You need to look at your self-esteem and consider what you are getting out of your life. Being active and positive is always great. Your life doesn't have to be a total downer if you are careful and thoughtful.

You must look at how you are surrounding yourself with good people while also thinking about the small victories in your life. Be ready to add a bit of variety to your life as well. Never think about the bad things in life or put yourself down all that quickly. The strategies you use to make a real difference if your life will add a special meaning to your world when used right.

Be certain that you use these ideal points when you are aiming to get the most out of your life. You will discover that your experiences do not have to be anywhere as difficult as you might think they have to be. More importantly, you will see that life is worth living and that there will always be great things to look forward to no matter what.

Your life will be bound to improve as you stick with the lessons you have learned in this guide. Everyone has to start from something and be ready to stay forward and ready for anything that can come along within your right.

**Your Gift!**

We want to show our appreciation that you support our work,
so we have put together a gift for you.


bit.ly/2u7pdNL


Just visit the link above to download it now.


We know you will love this gift.
Thanks!